D1604858

ECOLOGY

THE DELICATE BALANCE OF LIFE ON EARTH

ECOLOGY

THE DELICATE BALANCE OF LIFE ON EARTH

EDITED BY SHERMAN HOLLAR

Britannica
Educational Publishing
IN ASSOCIATION WITH

ROSEN
EDUCATIONAL SERVICES

Published in 2012 by Britannica Educational Publishing
(a trademark of Encyclopædia Britannica, Inc.)
in association with Rosen Educational Services, LLC
29 East 21st Street, New York, NY 10010.

First Edition

Britannica Educational Publishing
Michael I. Levy: Executive Editor, Encyclopædia Britannica
J.E. Luebering: Director, Core Reference Group, Encyclopædia Britannica
Adam Augustyn: Assistant Manager, Encyclopædia Britannica

Anthony L. Green: Editor, Compton's by Britannica
Michael Anderson: Senior Editor, Compton's by Britannica
Sherman Hollar: Associate Editor, Compton's by Britannica

Marilyn L. Barton: Senior Coordinator, Production Control
Steven Bosco: Director, Editorial Technologies
Lisa S. Braucher: Senior Producer and Data Editor
Yvette Charboneau: Senior Copy Editor
Kathy Nakamura: Manager, Media Acquisition

Rosen Educational Services
Jeanne Nagle: Senior Editor
Nelson Sá: Art Director
Cindy Reiman: Photography Manager
Karen Huang: Photo Researcher
Matthew Cauli: Designer, Cover Design
Introduction by Jeanne Nagle

Library of Congress Cataloging-in-Publication Data

Ecology : the delicate balance of life on earth / edited by Sherman Hollar.
    p. cm. — (The environment: ours to save)
"In association with Britannica Educational Publishing, Rosen Educational Services."
Includes bibliographical references and index.
ISBN 978-1-61530-507-0 (library binding)
1. Ecology—Juvenile literature. 2. Environmentalism—Juvenile literature. I. Hollar, Sherman.
QH541.14.E27 2011
577—dc22

                                                                            2010052490

Manufactured in the United States of America

Cover (front and back), p. 3 Shutterstock.com; interior background © www.istockphoto.com/Pawel Gaul

CONTENTS

There was a time, many years ago, when observing nature was an activity best left to farmers and poets. To protect their livelihoods, the former needed to keep an eye on weather events and the cycle of the seasons, not to mention the nearby wildlife that might make a meal out of their livestock. The latter was concerned mainly with the aesthetics, or surface beauty, of the natural world. Then, in 1869, a German scientist named Ernst Haeckel gave a name that lent credence to such watchfulness and musings. Thus the science of ecology was born.

Studying the interaction among living things and their environments is what ecology is all about. To do so requires a joining together of several branches of science. Biology, climatology, geology, and zoology all have their place in the ecological realm. Each branch offers vital information on

Various denizens of Namibia's Etosha National Park gather at a watering hole. Such species interaction and adaptability within a given environment is the crux of ecology. Shutterstock.com

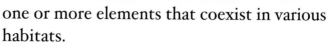

one or more elements that coexist in various habitats.

Every inhabitant must be accounted for because each has a role to play. The subtitle of this book is right on target. Life on Earth is a balancing act, one so delicate that any disruption to even the smallest living or nonliving element can have a ripple effect, upsetting the balance in several areas. As shown in these pages, ecologists use applied methodology and experimentation to examine activity within the various types of life groups. Doing so allows them to figure out if everything is running smoothly and identify where trouble spots might occur.

How ecologists study the environment also requires a multipronged approach. For scientific purposes, the Earth is divided into several life-sustaining layers. The largest is the biosphere, which is the thin, life-supporting stratum of Earth's surface. The biosphere can be broken down into major life zones called biomes. But in order to fully understand how plants and creatures interact with one another, ecologists break things down even further. The majority of ecologists focus their studies on a smaller scale, at the population, community, and ecosystem levels.

At the population level, ecologists study interactions within one particular species. They can gauge the balance of various populations by observing the size, density, and distribution of each. Communities provide details of how two or more species interact, and what effect this has on the community as a whole. The examination of ecosystems shows how species of plants and animals interact with their physical surroundings. The flow of energy and nutrient cycling are the two most important factors at this level.

A lot has changed since Haeckel first coined the term "ecology." As threats such as pollution, species extinction, and global warming have cast their long shadows over the planet, the ecological sciences have grown in importance, becoming a linchpin in international efforts to maintain and restore the environment to its natural state. Most likely ecology will be providing clues to the stability of the natural world for some time to come. After all, the life of every organism on Earth may very well hang in the balance.

CHAPTER 1
THE NATURE
OF ECOLOGY

The study of the ways in which organisms interact with their environment is called ecology. The word "ecology" was coined in 1869 by the German zoologist Ernst Haeckel, who derived it from the Greek *oikos*, which means "household." Economics is derived from the same word. However, economics deals with human "housekeeping," while ecology concerns the "housekeeping" of the natural world.

For many years most people did not consider ecology to be an important or even a real science. By the late 20th century, however, ecology had emerged as one of the most popular and important areas of biology. The effect of the environment on the organisms that inhabit it and vice versa is now acknowledged as a key element in a wide range of issues, including population growth, climate change, environmental pollution, species extinction, and human health and medicine.

Many public health specialists are incorporating an ecological component in

Ernest Haeckel. **Hulton Archive/Getty Images**

programs to control infectious diseases. For example, the rapid spread of West Nile virus (WNV) in the United States in the early 21st century resulted from the interaction of environmental factors with human and animal populations. Mosquitoes spread the virus by biting infected birds and then biting humans and other animals. One study in Florida noted that the number of WNV cases was especially high for years in which a dry spring season was followed by an especially wet summer. Further studies of environmental factors suggested that the limited water resources resulting from a dry spring may drive mosquitoes to congregate in isolated patches of dense vegetation where conditions remain humid. These humid patches also serve as nesting sites for an array of wild birds. In the close quarters of this temporary home, mosquitoes feed on and infect more birds than usual. When conditions change and the mosquitoes break out of their groupings and scatter, more people than usual will be bitten by these mosquitoes and become infected.

Such insights, gained from recognizing environmental factors promoting infection and transmission, are crucial for fighting

Mosquitoes spread the West Nile virus by biting infected birds, then biting humans. **Chris Johns/National Geographic Image Collection/ Getty Images**

WNV and many other diseases. If the ecology of the organisms is known, scientists can use an environmental approach to disrupt infection and the transmission of infectious diseases while treating and preventing the disease through medication and vaccination. This is but one example of the numerous ways in which scientists rely on an understanding of the complex interactions and interdependencies of living things and their environments.

EARLY STUDIES OF THE NATURAL WORLD

Long before the science of ecology was established, people in many occupations were aware of natural events and interactions.

A gaggle of geese migrating south is a natural harbinger of impending winter. Shutterstock.com

Early humans knew that gulls hovering over the water marked the position of a school of fish. Before the use of calendars to mark time, people used natural cues to guide seasonal endeavors. For instance, corn (maize) was planted when oak leaves were a certain size, and the sight of geese flying south was a warning to prepare for winter.

Until about 1850, the scientific study of such phenomena was called natural history, and a person who studied this was called a naturalist. As natural history became subdivided into special fields, such as geology, zoology, and botany, naturalists began incorporating laboratory work with field studies. This multidisciplinary approach gradually led to the establishment of ecology as a distinct field of study.

MODERN-DAY ECOLOGY

The modern study of ecology encompasses many areas of science. In addition to a solid understanding of biology, ecologists must also have some knowledge of weather and climate patterns, rock and mineral types, soil, and water. Familiarity with mathematics and statistics is essential. Whereas the

A Swiss scientist examines the effects of ozone on various plants via an open-top chamber in a laboratory. Sam Abell/ National Geographic Image Collection/Getty Images

study of natural history was largely based on observation and record-keeping, today most ecological studies center around rigorous experimentation requiring testable hypotheses and statistical analysis.

Ecologists supplement their study of actual habitats with both computer models and laboratory experiments. In the laboratory, ecologists can construct environmental chambers in which they can control the temperature, humidity, light, and other variables. They can then change one or more of these variables in specific, controlled ways and see how this affects plants, animals, and other organisms they establish in the chambers.

INTERDEPENDENCE IN NATURE

Ecology emphasizes the dependence of every form of life on other living things and on the natural resources in its environment, such as air, soil, and water. The English biologist Charles Darwin noted this interdependence when he wrote:

> *It is interesting to contemplate a tangled bank, clothed with many plants of many kinds, with birds singing on the bushes, with various insects flitting about, and with worms crawling through the damp earth, and to reflect that these elaborately constructed forms, so different from each other, and so dependent upon each other in so complex a manner, have all been produced by laws acting around us.*

Charles Darwin. Henry Guttmann/Hulton Archive/Getty Images

Darwin's observations of the relationship between organisms and their environment formed a key element in his theory of natural selection.

The term "environment" in ecology refers to both the physical and biological factors affecting organisms. The physical environment consists of abiotic, or nonliving, factors. These include resources such as light, carbon dioxide, oxygen, and soil; physical characteristics such as atmospheric pressure, temperature, and rainfall; and natural disturbances such as fire or tsunamis. The biological environment is made up of biotic factors—anything that is living or was living, as well as things that are immediately related to life. For example, the biotic factors in a forest include all of the organisms living in it—plants, animals, fungi, and microbes—as well as animal droppings, leaf litter, and rotting logs.

INTERACTIONS AT DIFFERENT SCALES

The interactions between living things and their environments occur at different scales. The most basic of these is the interaction between an individual organism and its environment.

NATURAL SELECTION

Struggling and living or dying could not lead to evolution if all members of each living kind or species were exactly alike. Charles Darwin found that members of a single species vary greatly in shape, size, color, strength, and so on. He also believed that most of these variations could be inherited.

Under the constant struggle to exist, organisms with harmful variations are more likely to die before they can reproduce. On average, living things with useful variations are more likely to survive and bear young and thus to pass on their helpful variations. When their descendants vary still more, the process is repeated. In other words, the struggle for existence selects organisms with helpful variations but makes others die out. Darwin called this process natural selection.

Over the ages, Darwin believed, changes from natural selection produce a slow succession of new plants, animals, and other organisms. These changes have enabled living things to go into all sorts of environments and become fitted, or adapted, to many different types of life. Darwin called his theory descent by modification, because he proposed that all living things were descended from earlier forms.

The largest scale is the biosphere, which consists of the relatively thin layers of Earth's air, soil, and water that are capable of supporting life together with all organisms that live there. The biosphere extends from roughly 6 miles (10 kilometers) above Earth's surface to the deep-sea vents of the ocean. The biosphere is divided into large regions called biomes (or major life zones) that are distinguished by climate and vegetation patterns. Most studies in ecology focus on interactions taking place at scales that fall in between the extremes of individuals and the biosphere: populations, communities, and ecosystems.

CHAPTER 2
POPULATIONS

A population consists of all of the individuals of the same species living within a given area. The area can be as small as a city park or as large as an ocean. For example, the polar bears that live in the area near Thunder Bay, Ontario, form a population, as do the saguaro cacti inhabiting the Sonoran desert, the maple trees growing in a particular city, and the *E. coli* bacteria living in a person's large intestine.

Ecologists who study populations are interested in how the population members interact with one another and with their environment. Many factors, from the size of the population to its spatial arrangement, play a role in these relationships.

POPULATION CHARACTERISTICS

Populations are characterized by several attributes. Among these are size, density, distribution, and life-history strategies.

An ecologist examines a field populated by poppies.
Monty Rakusen/Cultura/Getty Images

SIZE

The size of a population is defined simply as the number of individuals in that population at a given time. Population size is determined by four factors: the number of births, the number of deaths, the amount of immigration (the movement of individuals into one population from another), and the amount of emigration (the movement of individuals out

of a population) experienced by the population. Most ecologists study these factors as rates—the number of events per unit time. For example, birth rate is generally expressed as the number of births per year.

Births and immigration increase population size, while deaths and emigration lower it. When all of these factors are balanced, population size is at equilibrium. However, most populations in nature are dynamic—that is, they are always increasing or decreasing in size. Changes in population size are connected to many factors, from the availability of resources in the environment to certain innate species characteristics such as life-history strategies.

DENSITY

Population density is a measure of the number of individuals within a given area. Assuming that the population remains within the same area, the density then increases or decreases as the population size grows or falls, respectively.

Some organisms, such as bees, are adapted to living in high-density populations. Others, such as brown bears and alley cats, live in low-density populations. The latter is typical of animals that mark their territory.

Bees live and work in high-density populations. Shutterstock.com

DISTRIBUTION

The spatial arrangement of population members reveals much about how they live and interact with their environment. The way a population is spaced across an area is driven largely by food supply and other resources.

Ecologists have described three distinct distribution patterns based on how key resources are distributed. In a random distribution, individuals are scattered randomly

Spatial Distribution Patterns

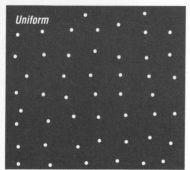

Uniform

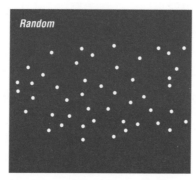

Random

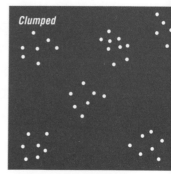

Clumped

Encyclopædia Britannica, Inc.

across a landscape without any particular pattern. Random distributions result when resources are distributed evenly or sporadically. They are very uncommon in nature. Examples include tropical fig trees, which are distributed sporadically most likely because their seeds are dispersed by fig-eating bats, and dandelions, which are wind-dispersed.

Uniform, or even, distribution patterns are common where there is strong competition for a limited resource. The scarcity of water drives the uniform spacing of desert shrubs, while competition for light produces the uniform spacing of redwood trees. Animals that display strong territorial behavior, such as stray cats, also tend to be distributed uniformly.

Clumped distributions are observed when resources are patchy or because of social structures. For example, the sporadic distribution of watering holes in the African savanna influences the clumped distribution of elephants. The strong social bonds of elephants, bees, and gorillas require a clumped distribution.

LIFE-HISTORY STRATEGIES

The life history of a species concerns the relationship between the age at which reproduction occurs and the age at death. Ecologists have observed two major life-history strategies that represent a trade-off between the amount of energy and resources "invested" in reproduction versus the amount invested in the parent itself. Such investment is not a conscious decision, of course, but rather an adaptation that has evolved over time. Both strategies maximize evolutionary fitness—the number of offspring that survive to have offspring of their own. Which strategy is followed depends on the species and the normal circumstances in which it exists.

At one extreme are opportunistic, or r-selected, species (the letter r represents the growth rate in statistics). Opportunistic species inhabit highly variable and unstable

Flowers and other opportunistic vegetation spring to life amid the charred remains of a forest in California's Sequoia National Forest. **David McNew/Getty Images**

environments, such as newly burned forests or marine tide pools. Life and death are unpredictable in such settings. There are not many resources to fight over in such locations, so fewer predators live there. The fewer the predators, the less chance there is that opportunistic species will become prey. Opportunistic plants and animals in such a setting can then concentrate primarily on having as many offspring as possible as early as possible, thus ensuring the survival of the species.

LIMITING FACTORS

Even when birth rates and immigration are high and resources are plentiful, population growth cannot continue unchecked, because resources are limited in the natural world. Most populations will increase in size until one or more crucial resources in their habitat are exhausted. At that point, the population size will decrease until it reaches its carrying capacity.

Factors that control population size are called limiting factors. Ecologists divide these into two categories: density-independent and density-dependent factors. Density-independent factors affect the same proportion of individuals in a population regardless of population size. Forest fires, severe storms, volcanic eruptions, acid rain, and climate changes are examples of density-independent factors. Density-dependent factors intensify as population size increases and become less intense as population size drops. For example, diseases transmitted through the air, such as tuberculosis, spread faster in dense populations than in sparse populations. Competition for food, shelter, mates, and other resources is another density-dependent factor that regulates populations, as is predation.

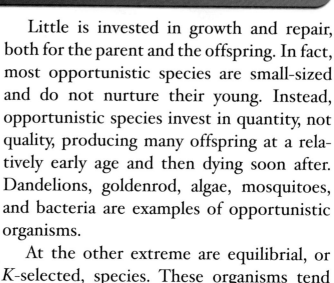

Little is invested in growth and repair, both for the parent and the offspring. In fact, most opportunistic species are small-sized and do not nurture their young. Instead, opportunistic species invest in quantity, not quality, producing many offspring at a relatively early age and then dying soon after. Dandelions, goldenrod, algae, mosquitoes, and bacteria are examples of opportunistic organisms.

At the other extreme are equilibrial, or *K*-selected, species. These organisms tend to remain near their carrying capacity (the maximum number of individuals the environment can support, symbolized by the letter *K*). They inhabit relatively stable environments in which survival depends on the ability to compete successfully for resources. Consequently, equilibrial species invest in quality, not quantity: they are larger than opportunists, live longer, reproduce later, and have fewer offspring. Some familiar equilibrial organisms include gorillas, elephants, trees, and humans.

POPULATION FLUCTUATIONS

Populations of some species show regular cycles of increase and decrease over several

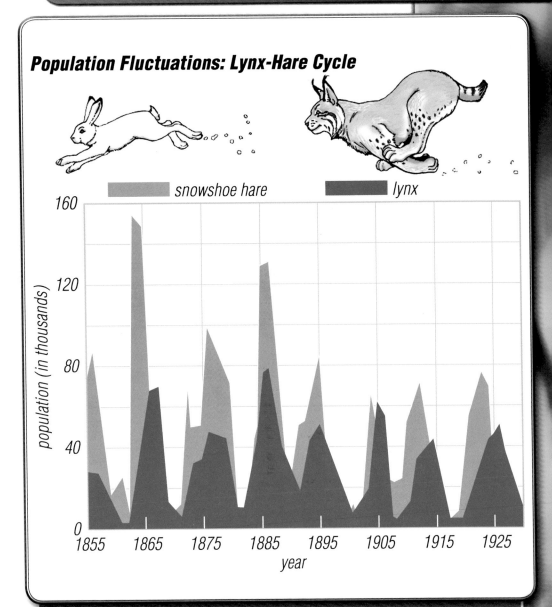

Population Fluctuations: Lynx-Hare Cycle

snowshoe hare | lynx

The Canada snowshoe hare population and lynx population show regular cycles of increase and decrease spanning many years. **Encyclopædia Britannica, Inc.**

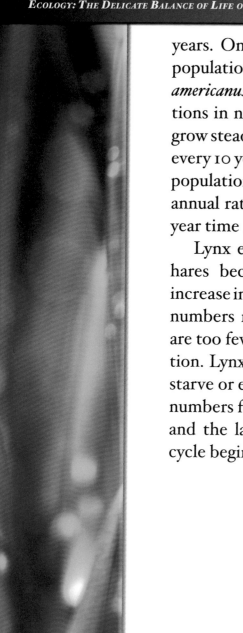

years. One such example is the fluctuating population cycles of snowshoe hare (*Lepus americanus*) and lynx (*Lynx canadensis*) populations in northern Canada. Hare populations grow steadily, reaching peak numbers roughly every 10 years, and then sharply decline. Lynx populations increase at roughly the same annual rate as hares, but with a one- to two-year time lag.

Lynx eat larger numbers of hares as the hares become more common, causing an increase in the latter's population size. As lynx numbers rise, hare numbers fall until there are too few hares to support the lynx population. Lynx numbers slowly fall as individuals starve or emigrate to other areas. While lynx numbers fall, there is less predation on hares, and the latter increase in number, and the cycle begins again.

CHAPTER 3
ECOLOGICAL COMMUNITIES

A community is made up of interacting groups of species living in a common location. The members of the community are connected through a network of interactions in which a direct interaction between two species may indirectly affect the community as a whole.

Certain types of plants and animals live together in similar communities regardless of their location on Earth. For example, antelope and other grazing mammals inhabit dry grasslands. Songbirds migrate seasonally from northern temperate woodlands of oak and maple to southern tropical forests. Marine tide pools contain algae, crustaceans, and mollusks.

Some communities are populated by species unique to that area. American bison (buffalo) and prairie dogs are unique to the grasslands of North America, while platypuses are found only in the waterways of Australia.

A herd of bison, which are indigenous to North America. **Panoramic Images/Getty Images**

CHARACTERISTICS OF COMMUNITIES

Like populations, communities and the way they function are affected by the presence and interplay of several factors. These include the diversity of the species in the community, the functional roles that the species play, and the presence of dominant species and those that have a disproportionately large impact on the community.

BIODIVERSITY

A high level of biodiversity, or biological diversity, is generally the sign of a healthy, well-functioning natural community. Biodiversity is often measured as the number of species within a given area. Some habitats have a modest amount of biodiversity while others, such as rainforests and coral reefs, are extremely rich in species. Long-term studies have shown that species-rich communities recover faster from disturbances than communities with low diversity. In the midwestern United States, grasslands with higher biodiversity were more drought-resistant compared to species-poor grasslands. Likewise, grasslands in the Serengeti region of eastern Africa that had greater species richness were able to recover better after grazing by animals than grasslands with fewer species.

Low biodiversity is a characteristic of artificial "communities," such as croplands and wide expanses of lawn. Natural

A frog rests on a patch of algae. Pollution in lakes causes algae and potentially harmful microorganisms to grow rapidly, creating a bloom. Shutterstock.com

communities that have become polluted often exhibit low species diversity. For example, a lake polluted with industrial and agricultural wastes such as sewage, detergents, and fertilizers may undergo eutrophication, which is an increase in concentrations of phosphorous, nitrogen, and other plant nutrients. The excessive amount of nutrients allows certain species of microscopic organisms or algae to grow on the lake's surface in much greater numbers. "Blooms" of some microbes may release harmful chemicals into the water. In addition, the mat of surface organisms blocks out much of the sunlight that would normally penetrate the water and also eventually causes the water to become deficient in oxygen. Species of fish and other underwater organisms may then die.

NICHE

In ecology, a niche is the functional role played by a species in the community it inhabits: where it lives, what it eats and recycles, and what preys on it. A community may have millions of different niches, all of which are connected and all of which must be occupied for the community to function effectively. Only one species can occupy a niche. Two species trying to fill the same niche must compete for it, with one species eventually outcompeting the other.

When a species goes extinct, its niche becomes empty, and many species will compete to fill it. Many niches become available

following mass extinction events and are rapidly filled by surviving species that have adaptations that allow them to take over the niche.

Just as all niches in a community must be filled, all species in a community must have a niche. If a niche becomes lost or changes because of a disturbance such as an earthquake or fire, the species that had occupied it must emigrate or try to adapt by occupying another niche (for which it has to outcompete the species occupying it). If this fails, the species will probably die out within the community.

DOMINANCE

In most communities, the growth or behavior of one or more species controls the activity and other characteristics of the community. Such species are called dominants. The dominant species in a forest may be a certain tree species whose growth may affect the amount of light available to other species. One of the dominant microbes in the human mouth is *Streptococcus salivarius*. Dominant species influence community diversity as well as stability.

Animal Dominance Hierarchy

Scientists have found that many groups of animals, most notably baboons, birds, foxes, lions, and crocodiles, establish dominance hierarchies. The best-known example is the pecking order of chickens. Flock members are arranged on the "rungs" of a social ladder, with each chicken superior to those below and subordinate to those above. The top animal has primary access to the necessities of life, such as the best food, mates, and living quarters. Submissive animals are left with less-desirable food, mates, and living quarters. Such animals may even be expected to groom dominant members and to help care for the offspring of more dominant animals, because subordinates are often prevented from having offspring of their own.

In other animal groups, dominance hierarchies are more complicated. Wolf packs, for example, are led by two dominants who have three subclasses of subordinates below them. Other animals have only one dominant leader with all other animals below him or her being exactly equal. Once an animal has established dominance, challenges to the order are rarely made from within the group, since animals are reluctant to fight other animals that are

bigger, stronger, or more aggressive than they are themselves. Sometimes, however, animals from outside the group can successfully challenge and overthrow a longtime leader, but this is rare.

In more intelligent species, such as baboons, factors beyond mere size and strength determine the dominance hierarchy. Age seniority, hormonal condition, maternal lineage, and personality are sometimes factors that affect dominance in more intelligent animals. In baboon groups, furthermore, hierarchies are often elaborate. Adult males are dominant over less mature males and females, yet a fully mature female can be dominant over a less mature male. A dominant baboon displays its superiority with rapid "fencing" maneuvers, open-jaw displays, hitting, and other aggressive behavior.

KEYSTONE SPECIES

The presence of a keystone species is crucial to maintaining the functioning and diversity of many communities. A keystone species is a species that has an unusually large effect on its neighbors. Through predation or competition it may prevent the overgrowth of a population that would otherwise dominate the community. This is the case in the rocky intertidal

Sea stars, more commonly known as starfish, are gathered in an Arches, Washington, tidal pool. Brandon Cole/Visuals Unlimited/Getty Images

pools found on the Pacific Northwest coast of North America in which the sea star *Pisaster ochraceus* is the keystone species. *Pisaster* preys on the mussel *Mytilus californianus*, keeping the mussel population from getting too large. When ecologists removed *Pisaster* experimentally, the *Mytilus* population grew so rapidly that it outcrowded every other species that normally inhabited the community.

In some communities, the keystone species provides critical resources for other members of the community. Because they provide fruit year-round, fig trees (*Ficus* species) in the tropical rainforests of Central and South America provide fruit for many birds and other animals during periods in which other fruits are scarce. Without the fig trees, many animals in these communities would have to emigrate to other habitats, thereby decreasing community diversity.

ADAPTATION

Certain animals and plants develop characteristics that help them cope with their environment better than others of their species. This natural biological process is called adaptation. Among the superior traits developed through adaptation are those that may

help in obtaining food or shelter, in providing protection, and in producing and protecting offspring. The better adapted organisms then tend to thrive, reproduce, and pass their heritable variations along to their progeny better than those without the superior characteristics. This is called natural selection. It results in the evolution of more and more organisms that are better fitted to their environments.

Each living thing is adapted to its mode of life in a general way, but each is adapted especially to its own distinct niche. A plant, for example, depends upon its roots to anchor itself and to absorb water and inorganic chemicals. It depends upon its green leaves for photosynthesis, the process of using the sun's energy to manufacture food from inorganic chemicals. These are general adaptations, common to most plants. In addition, there are special adaptations that only certain species of plants possess. The mistletoe, for example, is a parasitic plant; it lacks true roots but lives with its rootlike *haustoria* buried in the branches of a tree. It depends upon the tree to anchor itself and to absorb water and inorganic chemicals. In order to survive, the mistletoe must establish its parasitic relationship with a suitable tree. The mistletoe is also dependent upon an insect to pollinate its flowers, and a

43

bird to spread its seeds by eating the berries and depositing its droppings that contain the seeds onto the branches of appropriate trees.

Many animals have adaptations that help them elude their predators. Some insects are camouflaged by their body color or shape, and many resemble a leaf or a twig. The coats

A fawn gains protection against predators from its ability to remain still and from its dappled coat that blends into the background. **Leonard Lee Rue III**

of deer are colored to blend with their sur-roundings. Their behavior, too, is adaptive; they have the ability to remain absolutely still when an enemy is near. These adaptations arose from the natural selection of heritable variations.

Organisms have a great variety of ways of adapting. They may adapt in their structure, function, and genetics; in their locomotion or dispersal for defense and attack; in their reproduction and development; and in other respects. Favorable adaptations may involve migration for survival under certain conditions of temperature, for example. An organism may create its own environment; warm-blooded mammals have the ability to adjust body heat precisely to maintain their ideal tempera-ture despite changing weather. Adaptations to temporary situations may be reversible, as when humans become suntanned.

Usually adaptations are an advantage, but sometimes an organism is so well adapted to a particular environment that, if condi-tions change, it finds it difficult or impossible to readapt to the new conditions. The huia bird of New Zealand, for example, depended upon a close collaboration between male and female: the male chiseled holes in decay-ing wood with its stout beak, and the female reached in with her long, slender beak to capture grubs. When New Zealand was deforested, these birds could no longer feed in their accustomed way and soon became extinct.

ABIOTIC INFLUENCES ON COMMUNITIES

The makeup of a community is largely determined by abiotic factors such as climate and

Squat pine trees and daisies grow in the semi-arid climate of Arizona.
Jim Steinfeldt/Michael Ochs Archives/Getty Images

46

rainfall. In terrestrial communities, vegetation patterns are influenced by climate and soil. Climate has a marked effect on the height of dominant native plants. For instance, the humid climate of the eastern United States supports tall forest trees. Westward from Minnesota and Texas, the change in climate from subhumid to semiarid favors the growth of squatty, scattered trees and tall grasses or thickets. As the climate becomes drier, tall-grass prairies dominate. The harsh, arid conditions at the eastern base of the Rockies support the dominant short-grass steppe.

Changes in elevation also are reflected in changes of climate and humidity. At very high altitudes in the Rockies, alpine rangelands exist above the timberline. Here, the climatic factor of cold outweighs that of moisture, and tundra vegetation similar to that of the Arctic regions is nurtured. In the basins west of the Rockies, the desert scrub typical of arid climates prevails. The intense moisture and cool climate of the coastal Pacific Northwest supports the lush, temperate rainforests typical of the area.

CHAPTER 4
COMMUNITY INTERACTIONS AND ECOLOGICAL SUCCESSIONS

The organization and stability of a biological community results from the interactions between its member species. The structure of a community is constantly changing, however. The change of biological communities over time is known as succession, or ecological succession.

INTERACTIONS BETWEEN SPECIES

Each interaction between two species directly affects each of them. These effects may be beneficial or detrimental, depending on the species and the interaction. Some interactions have a distinct effect on one species but no effect on another.

In addition to their direct effects, some interactions between two species have indirect effects on other members of the community. The connection between all of the direct and indirect effects forms an interactive web that binds the community together. There are four main types of species interactions: competition, predation, commensalism, and mutualism.

COMPETITION

The struggle between two or more individuals or species for a common resource is called competition. It is a characteristic of all communities and one of the most basic interactions in life.

A hyena battles several vultures for an animal carcass in the African Serengeti. **Franz Aberham/Photographer's Choice/Getty Images**

THE LONG-TERM EFFECTS OF COMPETITION

Competition exerts a strong direct effect on the competing individuals or species. Neither side benefits from competition since, in competing for a certain resource, each side is depriving the other of some share of it. Over evolutionary time competition can reshape the community, as some species emigrate or become extinct, while others evolve adaptations that may enable them to utilize a different resource.

Organisms may compete for several resources simultaneously, though usually one of these is the most critical. This is called the limiting resource because it limits the population growth of both competing species.

Competition may be interspecific (between members of different species) or intraspecific (between individuals of the same species). Examples of interspecific competition include hyenas and vultures that compete for carcasses, birds competing for nesting sites, and plant roots in dry rangelands that compete for water. Intraspecific competition also occurs over resources such as food or water; it also is common during the mating season as individuals compete for mates.

PREDATION AND OTHER
FEEDING METHODS

The capturing, killing, and eating of one living organism by another is called predation. The organism that consumes is called a predator; the organism that is consumed is the prey. Like competition, predation is one of the driving forces that shape communities. By preying on other organisms, predators help to regulate population sizes. Predation is also an important factor in natural selection—prey that can be captured by predators are less fit in an evolutionary sense. This does not mean they are physically weak or inferior, though sometimes that also plays a role. Evolutionary fitness is equivalent to reproductive success—therefore, an organism that can be captured and destroyed will not survive to reproduce and thus has a lower fitness relative to organisms that evade predation.

Predation also helps move energy and materials such as nitrogen and carbon through the community. Predation exerts a positive direct effect on the predator and a negative direct effect on the prey.

Herbivory, in which an animal consumes and destroys plants, and parasitism, in which

a parasite absorbs its nutrients from the host's body, are closely related to predation in principle. These feeding methods also have a positive direct effect on the feeder and a negative direct effect on the organism being fed upon; however, herbivores and parasites usually do not kill outright the organisms upon which they feed. A herbivore typically eats only part of a plant before moving on to another. While a parasite usually weakens its host, thereby negatively affecting its ability to survive, it also usually does not kill the host directly.

Herbivores range from large grazing mammals such as sheep and cattle to tiny ants and other insects. Large grazing mammals tend to feed on grasses and shrubs, while insect herbivores feed on and destroy leaves. Other types of grazers feed on fungi. Parasites may be bacteria, fungi, protozoa, or plants or animals. They are very common, perhaps accounting for as many as half of all species on Earth.

Predation, herbivory, and parasitism can coevolve over time as each side in the battle evolves and mounts an effective defense. In

A predatory snowy egret captures its prey, a frog.
Shutterstock.com

Wild horses, in the pastures of Bosnia's Krug Mountain, graze on tender blades of grass. Grazing is a form of herbivory. **Elvis Barukcic/ AFP/Getty Images**

this evolutionary "arms race," natural selection progressively escalates the defenses and counterdefenses of the species. The thick shells of mollusks in Lake Tanganyika and the powerful claws of the freshwater crabs that prey on them are thought to have coevolved through this process of escalation. Host species develop defenses against infections, and the parasites, in turn, adapt by gradually evolving resistance to these.

COMMENSALISM

In a commensal relationship, one species benefits while the other remains unaffected. The commensal organism may depend on its host for food, shelter, support, or transportation. One example is the relationship of remoras and sharks. By attaching itself to a shark, a remora is carried along on the shark's power. This allows the remora to "travel" to different areas without having to expend its own energy to swim. The shark is completely unaffected by the remora's presence.

Another example involves the tiny oyster crab (*Pinnotheres ostreum*). As a larva, the crab enters the shell of an oyster, receiving shelter while it grows. Once fully grown, however, the crab cannot exit through the narrow opening of the oyster's valves. It remains within the shell, snatching particles of food from the oyster but not harming its unwitting benefactor.

Another form of commensalism occurs between small plants called epiphytes and the large tree branches on which they grow.

A remora attaches itself to a leopard shark. **Douglas Faulkner**

Epiphytes depend on their hosts for structural support but do not derive nourishment from them or harm them in any way.

MUTUALISM

An interaction between two species that benefits both of them is called a mutualism.

Mutualistic interactions can be integral to the organization of biological communities; in some cases, they are among the most important elements of the community structure. Pollination and seed dispersal are two of the best studied mutualisms. In pollination, an animal—usually a bird or insect—feeds on the nectar or the pollen of a flower. As it feeds, some of the flower's pollen sticks

Closeup of a bee with pollen attached to its head and legs. Pollination benefits both the bee and the flower. Shutterstock.com

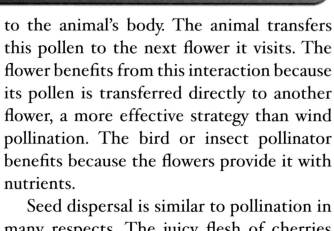

to the animal's body. The animal transfers this pollen to the next flower it visits. The flower benefits from this interaction because its pollen is transferred directly to another flower, a more effective strategy than wind pollination. The bird or insect pollinator benefits because the flowers provide it with nutrients.

Seed dispersal is similar to pollination in many respects. The juicy flesh of cherries and other fruits are an adaptation produced by the plant to attract animals. After a bird feeds on a fruit, it flies off and later regurgitates the seed, usually at some distance from the parent plant. The bird benefits from the nutrients in the fruit, while the plant benefits because its seed is carried away from the parent plant. This is adaptive for the plant in that an offspring that germinates from the seed will not be competing with its parent for resources, as it would if it simply fell from a branch on the parent tree to the ground below.

Many mutualisms have coevolved over time to the extent that one species cannot exist without the other. An example of this is the mutualism between termites and a protozoan species that lives in their guts. Although

A squirrel buries nuts in anticipation of the winter. Nuts that are over-looked as food stores germinate and become sapling trees and young plants. **Daniel King/Flickr/Getty Images**

termites feed on wood, they cannot digest it, but the protozoa in their guts can. The termites benefit by getting nutrients from a food source that few organisms compete for, while the protozoa get a place to live.

SUCCESSION

All communities are subject to periodic disturbances, ranging from events that have only localized effects, such as the loss of a tree that creates a gap in the canopy of a forest, to events of catastrophic consequences, including wildfires, violent storms, or volcanic eruptions. Each new disturbance within a landscape creates an opportunity for new species to colonize that region. In doing so, these new species also alter the character of the community, creating an environment that is suitable to even newer species. This is the process of ecological succession.

Two different types of succession have been distinguished: primary succession and secondary succession. Both create a continually changing mix of species within communities as the landscape is altered by different types of disturbances. The progression of species that evolve during both types of succession is not random, however. Both forms of succession proceed in a very ordered, sequential manner. Only a small number of species are capable of colonizing and thriving in a disturbed habitat. As new plant species colonize the habitat, they modify it by altering such things as the amount of shade on the ground or the mineral composition of the soil. These changes allow other species that are adapted to the changed habitat to invade and succeed the old species, which usually cannot live in the environment they themselves changed. The newer species are superseded, in turn, by still newer species. A similar succession of animal species occurs. Interactions between plants, animals, other living things, and the environment influence the pattern and rate of successional change.

PRIMARY SUCCESSION

While this general sequence holds true for both primary and secondary succession, the processes are distinguished by several key elements. The process of primary succession begins in essentially barren areas—regions in which the substrate (the surface or material forming the foundation of the area) cannot

sustain life. Lava flows, newly formed sand dunes, and rocks exposed by a retreating glacier are typical substrates from which primary succession begins. These barren substrates are colonized by pioneer organisms such as lichens that can live on the barren rocks and physically break them down, extracting minerals and providing organic matter as they die and decompose.

Over hundreds of years, the substrate gradually turns into soil that can support other plants, such as mosses and grasses. These plants in turn modify and stabilize the soil so that it can support shrubs and trees such as cottonwoods that cannot

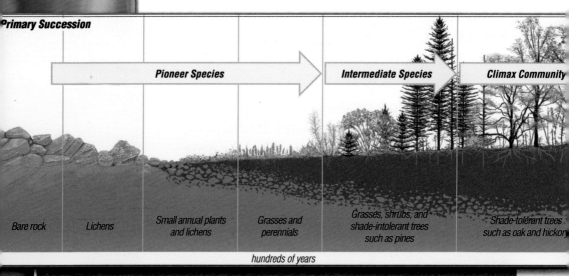

Primary Succession

Pioneer Species

Intermediate Species

Climax Community

| Bare rock | Lichens | Small annual plants and lichens | Grasses and perennials | Grasses, shrubs, and shade-intolerant trees such as pines | Shade-tolerant trees such as oak and hickory |

hundreds of years

The stages of primary succession. Encyclopædia Britannica, Inc.

tolerate shade. The presence of the shade-intolerant trees creates shade, however, allowing the colonization by other trees, such as jack pines.

The last stage of primary succession is the climax community, which is relatively stable. In most temperate areas, the climax community is a hardwood forest dominated by trees such as oak and hickory. In contrast to the pioneer community at the onset of succession, the climax community is more complex, composed of many different species occupying many niches.

SECONDARY SUCCESSION

The main difference between primary and secondary succession is that the latter occurs on soil that already exists—that is, in areas where a previously existing community has been removed, most often by disturbances that are relatively smaller in scale and that do not eliminate all life and nutrients from the environment. Secondary succession takes place following a major disturbance, such as a fire or flood. Farmland that has been abandoned also can undergo secondary succession.

A grassland wildfire or a storm that uproots trees within a forest create patches of habitat that are colonized by early successional species. Depending on the extent of the disturbance, some of these are original species that survived the disturbance. Other species may have recolonized the area from nearby habitats. Still other species may actually be released or "awakened" from a dormant condition by the disturbance. Many plant species in fire-prone environments have seeds that remain dormant within the soil until the heat of a fire stimulates them to germinate.

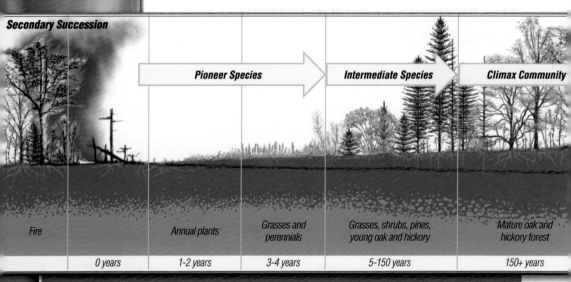

Secondary Succession

Pioneer Species → Intermediate Species → Climax Community

| Fire | Annual plants | Grasses and perennials | Grasses, shrubs, pines, young oak and hickory | Mature oak and hickory forest |
| 0 years | 1-2 years | 3-4 years | 5-150 years | 150+ years |

The stages of secondary succession. **Encyclopædia Britannica, Inc.**

Because soil does not have to be formed, secondary succession is considerably faster than primary succession. For example, the pioneer species colonizing an abandoned field might be weeds such as crabgrass. After a year or so, perennials and tall grasses will invade, followed several years later by pine seedlings. The latter will mature into a pine forest, which may stand for about 100 years before giving way to a climax community of hardwoods.

CHAPTER 5
ECOSYSTEMS

An ecosystem consists of a biological community and its physical environment. Terrestrial ecosystems include forests, savannas, grasslands, scrublands, tundras, and deserts. Marine and freshwater aquatic ecosystems include oceans, lakes, rivers, and wetlands. All of Earth's ecosystems together constitute the biosphere.

Ecosystems are categorized into abiotic (able to live without oxygen) and biotic (oxygen-dependent) components. Abiotic components include minerals, climate, soil, water, and sunlight. Biotic components of an ecosystem include all living members and associated entities such as carcasses and wastes. Together these constitute two major forces: the flow of energy through the ecosystem and the cycling of nutrients within the ecosystem.

PHOTOSYNTHESIS AND THE BIOSPHERE

The fundamental source of energy in almost all ecosystems is radiant energy emitted

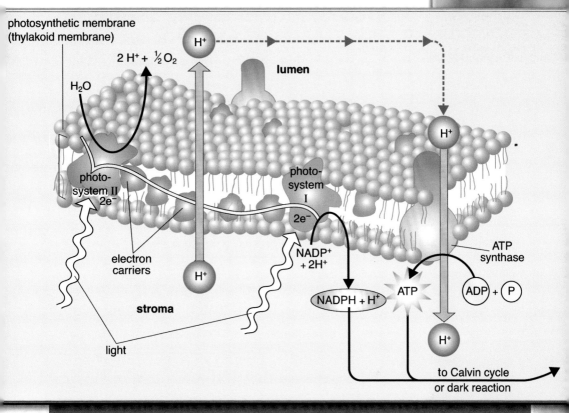

photosynthetic membrane
(thylakoid membrane)

$2 H^+ + \frac{1}{2}O_2$

H_2O

H⁺

lumen

photo-
system II
2e⁻

photo-
system
I

2e⁻

electron
carriers

H⁺

NADP⁺
+ 2H⁺

ATP
synthase

stroma

NADPH + H⁺

ATP

ADP + P

light

H⁺

to Calvin cycle
or dark reaction

An illustration of the process of photosynthesis. © **Merriam-Webster Inc.**

from the Sun. Most of the biosphere is based on the process of photosynthesis, by which plants and some microorganisms use sunlight to convert water, carbon dioxide (from the atmosphere), and minerals into oxygen (which then enters the atmosphere) and simple and complex sugars. Animals eat many of these plants and microorganisms, thus consuming much of their stored energy. Energy is concentrated further into a small number of carnivores, who eat other animals. Scavengers eat dead plants and animals.

After all of the above creatures die, they are gradually buried in the ground or sink to the seafloor. In this way, they are eventually incorporated into Earth's lithosphere, with some gases, such as methane, being released into the atmosphere or hydrosphere.

TROPHIC LEVELS

Biotic organisms of an ecosystem are linked through what they eat and what eats them. These are classified into three levels: producers, consumers, and decomposers. Producers are organisms that do not eat other living things to obtain energy and nutrients. They are also called autotrophs, meaning "self-nourishing." Most producers obtain energy and nutrients through photosynthesis, using energy from the Sun to convert carbon dioxide and water into simple sugars. The producer can then use the energy stored in these sugars to produce more complex compounds.

All green plants are producers that undergo photosynthesis, as are algae and certain kinds of microscopic organisms, such as cyanobacteria (formerly called blue-green algae).

CREATURES OF THE DARK

In recent decades, scientists have found ecosystems (groups of interdependent organisms and their environment) independent of sunlight. An example is the communities of creatures thriving around hydrothermal vents in the deep ocean. These vents spew hot water, laden with sulfur dioxide gas, from the ocean floor.

Tube worms. Shutterstock.com

Bacteria called chemoautotrophs make their food (sugars, as in photosynthesis) by using these hot gases along with carbon dioxide.

Other creatures, such as long, red tube worms, store the bacteria in their bodies and live off their energy. Bacteria that have been found in deep underground rocks may be using hydrogen to make their food. The hydrogen may come from water broken apart by the nuclear radiation from radioactive elements, such as uranium, trapped in the rock.

A second and much rarer kind of producer gets its energy not from sunlight but from chemicals, through a process called chemosynthesis. These producers include microscopic organisms living at extreme conditions at volcanic vents in the deep-sea floor and in rock deep underground.

All other living things—including all animals, all fungi, and many bacteria and other microorganisms—depend on producers as sources of energy and nutrients, either directly or indirectly. These forms of life are called heterotrophs, meaning "other-nourishing." They include consumers and decomposers. Neither can make their own food. Instead, consumers must feed on other organisms, including producers and other consumers. Most animals, for example, eat plants or other animals that have fed on plants. Decomposers feed on the tissues of dead or dying producers and consumers. Bacteria and fungi are common decomposers.

The producers, consumers, and decomposers in an ecosystem form several trophic, or feeding, levels in which organisms at one level feed on those from the level below and are themselves consumed by organisms at the level above. At the base of these trophic levels are the producers—by converting light energy or chemical energy into nutrients, producers essentially support the entire ecosystem. The next trophic level above the producers consists of the primary consumers. These generally are herbivores such as cows and other organisms that consume only plants or other producers. The next trophic level contains the secondary consumers—organisms that consume primary consumers as well as producers. Some ecosystems have more consumer levels—tertiary consumers, which feed on secondary consumers, and so on. The final link in all food chains is the

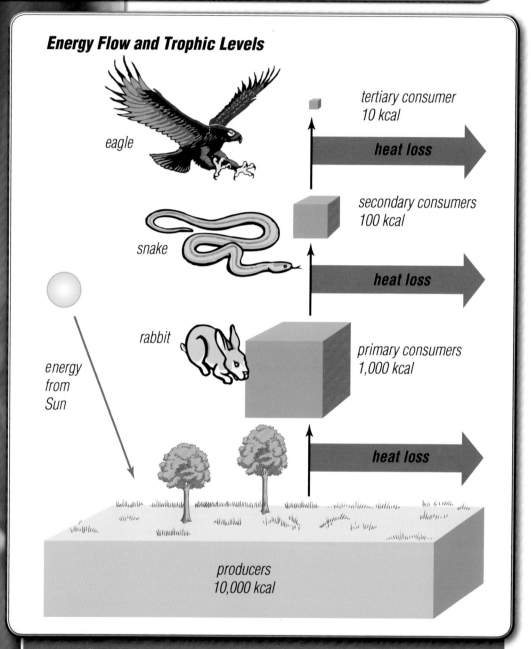

Energy Flow and Trophic Levels

eagle

tertiary consumer
10 kcal

heat loss

snake

secondary consumers
100 kcal

heat loss

rabbit

primary consumers
1,000 kcal

energy
from
Sun

heat loss

producers
10,000 kcal

Energy flow and trophic levels. **Encyclopædia Britannica, Inc.**

decomposers, which break down dead organisms and organic wastes.

The amount of energy at each trophic level decreases as it moves through an ecosystem. As little as 10 percent of the energy at any trophic level is transferred to the next level; the rest is lost largely through metabolic processes as heat. If a grassland ecosystem has 10,000 kilocalories (kcal) of energy concentrated in vegetation, only about 1,000 kcal will be transferred to primary consumers, and very little (only 10 kcal) will make it to the tertiary level. Energy pyramids such as this help to explain the trophic structure of an ecosystem. The number of consumer trophic levels that can be supported is dependent on the size and energy richness of the producer level.

Food Chains

The movement of organic matter and energy from the producer level through the trophic levels of an ecosystem makes up a food chain. A food chain is a single pathway connecting a producer with several levels of consumers. The levels of a food chain are essentially the same across ecosystems, though the organisms at each level differ. For example, a grassland food chain might include grasses (producers), field mice (primary consumers), snakes (secondary consumers), and hawks (tertiary consumers). A marine food chain

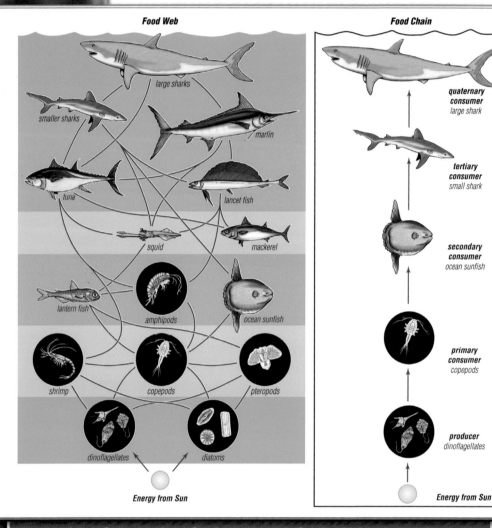

Examples of a marine food web and food chain. Encyclopædia Britannica, Inc.

might consist of algae (producers), copepods (primary consumers), sunfish (secondary consumers), small sharks (tertiary consumers), and large sharks (quaternary consumers). The consumers at the uppermost trophic level of any food chain are called top predators. As their name implies, they have no predators; instead, their population size is controlled through competition.

Most ecosystems have more than one food chain, which overlap and interconnect into a network called a food web. As energy moves through the ecosystem, much of it is lost at each trophic level. Similar proportions of energy are lost at every level of the food chain. That is, each successive trophic level has less energy than the level below it. This is the main reason that few food chains extend beyond five levels (from producer through decomposer): there is not enough energy available at higher trophic levels to support consumers occupying these.

NUTRIENT RECYCLING

Through plant growth and decay, water and carbon, nitrogen, and other elements are circulated in endless cycles through the ecosystem. Nutrients in soil, as well as the carbon

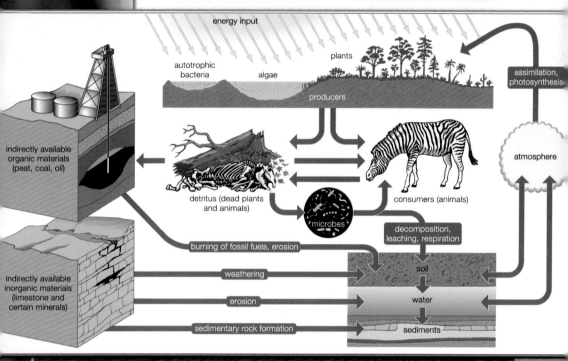

Biogeochemical cycle: energy and nutrients in the biosphere.
Encyclopaedia Britannica, Inc.

and oxygen from carbon dioxide, are incorporated into plant tissues. When the plant is consumed, these nutrients are passed to the consumer, which incorporates them into its tissues and ultimately passes them on to the next trophic level when it is itself consumed. Organisms that are not eaten die and transfer nutrients in their tissues to decomposers, which then recycle these into the ecosystem, where they become available to producers.

76

CONCLUSION

D ramatic changes in the biosphere have taken place over the course of the past 10,000 years. The invention of agriculture and animal husbandry and the eventual spread of these practices throughout the world have allowed humans to co-opt a large portion of the available productivity of Earth. Calculations show that humans currently use approximately 40 percent of the energy of the Sun captured by organisms on land. Use of such an inordinately large proportion of Earth's productivity by a single animal species is unique in the history of the planet. Accelerating population growth, climate change, and environmental pollution threaten to bring about major disruptions to the biosphere.

Despite enormous advances made over the past few decades toward understanding the biosphere, there is clearly much more to learn. Many would agree that we are just beginning to perceive the delicate nature of Earth's ecosystems and the

complex ecological processes that keep the biosphere hospitable to life. A more thorough understanding of the interactions and interdependencies of living things and their environments will help scientists to assess the impacts of the disruptions that occur and to address these problems effectively.

adaptation The process of species evolving the traits necessary for survival in their environment.

biodiversity In general, the variety of life found within an ecosystem or, more typically, the total variety of life on Earth.

biome The largest geographic biotic unit; a major community of plants and animals with similar life forms and environmental conditions.

biosphere The thin, life-supporting stratum of Earth's surface.

congregate To collect into a group or crowd.

dominance Prevalence of one over all others.

ecosystem A grouping of biota, their physical environment, and all their interrelationships in a particular unit of space.

equilibrial Existing in a state of balance.

hierarchy People or things arranged by ranks or class.

hydrosphere The aqueous envelope of the earth that includes the bodies of water and the water vapor in the atmosphere.

innate Existing in, belonging to, or determined by factors present in an individual from birth.

lithosphere The outer part of Earth, which is composed of solid rock.

migrate To move from one place to another.

opportunistic Relating to a microorganism that is usually harmless but which can spread disease when the host's resistance has been weakened.

parasitic The condition of living in or on another living organism in order to survive.

phenomena An observable fact or event.

pollinate To place pollen on the stigma of a flower.

predation A mode of life in which food is primarily obtained by the killing and consuming of animals.

progeny Offspring of animals or plants.

protozoa Single-celled organisms with a nucleus and other small organs.

regurgitate To throw or pour back as from a cavity, such as one's stomach.

scavenger An organism that typically feeds on refuse or dead meat.

spatial arrangement The way a population is spaced across an area.

sporadic Occurring occasionally, randomly, or at irregular instances.

territoriality The pattern of behavior associated with the defense of an animal's territory.

trophic Of or relating to nutrition.

Canadian Ecology Centre
6905 Hwy 17, P.O. Box 430
Mattawa, ON P0H1V0
Canada
(888) 747-7577
Web site: http://www.canadianecology.ca
The Canadian Ecology Centre offers online
research resources aimed at conservation
and development issues and the environment at large, as well as forestry and
mining. Hands-on activities and training
in outdoors skills are also available.

Earth Island Institute
2150 Allston Way, Suite 460
Berkeley, CA 94704-1375
(510) 859-9100
Web site: http://www.earthisland.org
Earth Island Institute is dedicated to con-
serving, preserving, and restoring Earth's
ecosystems. The organization spearheads
a number of environmental projects and
offers guidance and support for people
who want to take action in their own
communities.

Ecological Society of America
1990 M Street NW, Suite 700
Washington, DC 20036

(202) 833-8773

Web site: http://www.esa.org

The Ecological Society of America (ESA)
is a network of scientists who focus on
the study of ecology. The ESA provides
scholarships and youth programs in ecology and the natural sciences. The Web
site provides links to scientists and other
sites for more information as well as
access to the ESA's own projects.

Miistakis Institute
2500 University Drive NW, Room 2157
Calgary, AB T2N1N4
Canada
(403) 220-8968
Web site: http://www.rockies.ca/index.php
The Miistakis Institute has been involved
in many projects relating to research and
the development of tools for ecology
and land use. Online resources include
a library of datasets on land use impacts
and human-animal interactions.

Society for Ecological Restoration
1017 O Street NW
Washington, DC 20001
(202) 299-9518

Web site: http://www.ser.org

The Society for Ecological Restoration is a
nonprofit organization created to support those who are actively engaged
in ecologically-sensitive repair and
management of ecosystems. Through
conferences, publications, and awards
programs, the Society raises awareness
of, and encourages research in, ecological
restoration.

WEB SITES

Due to the changing nature of Internet links,
Rosen Educational Services has developed an
online list of Web sites related to the subject
of this book. This site is updated regularly.
Please use this link to access the list:

http://www.rosenlinks.com/teos/ecol

Cain, Michael L., and others. *Ecology* (Sinauer Associates, 2008).

Freeman, Jennifer. *Ecology* (Collins, 2007).

Fullick, Ann. *Feeding Relationships* (Heinemann, 2006).

Gibson, J.P., and Gibson, T.R. *Plant Ecology* (Chelsea House, 2006).

Krasny, Marianne, and others. *Invasion Ecology*, student ed. (NSTA Press, 2003).

Leuzzi, Linda. *Life Connections: Pioneers in Ecology* (Franklin Watts, 2000).

Quinlan, S.E. *The Case of the Monkeys that Fell from the Trees: And Other Mysteries in Tropical Nature* (Boyds Mills, 2003).

Scott, Michael. *The Young Oxford Book of Ecology* (Oxford Univ. Press, 1998).

Slobodkin, L.B. *A Citizen's Guide to Ecology* (Oxford Univ. Press, 2003).

Ziegler, Christian, and Leigh, E.G. *A Magic Web: The Forest of Barro Colorado Island* (Oxford Univ. Press, 2002).